RING OF GULLIO

Area of Outstanding Natural Beauty

On the 18th December 1991, the Department of the Environment (NI) made an Order designating the Ring of Gullion Area of Outstanding Natural Beauty (AONB). This designation gives formal statutory recognition to the quality of the landscape centered around Slieve Gullion and within the geologically unique Ring of Gullion hills.

**ENVIRONMENT
SERVICE**

Acknowledgements: Large format photography by Robert Thompson.

Printed in United Kingdom for HMSO
Dd. 0303184, C20, 12/91, 29254

CONTENTS

PREFACE

The Ring of Gullion, in South Armagh, has a remarkable countryside and a fascinating history. Its special landscape, wildlife and heritage features reflect the complex physical structure of the rocks and the way the area has been farmed for thousands of years. The heather clad Slieve Gullion mountain towers over farmland minutely divided by walls and hedges. The feeling of enclosure is emphasized by the outer ring of rugged hills, their contrasting land use and vegetation closely reflecting the topography. Heritage features are abundant and illustrate episodes in past life in the area — the gateway to Ulster.

In designating the Ring of Gullion Area of Outstanding Natural Beauty (AONB) the Department of the Environment formally recognises that Slieve Gullion and its surrounding farmland and ring of hills, is a landscape of national importance. The purpose of designation is to help protect and where possible improve this landscape for the benefit of those people living in the area and for the visitors who come to see and enjoy the beautiful countryside.

The aim of this Guide is to describe the reasons for designation of the Ring of

Slieve Gullion from Cloghinny

Gullion AONB, to bring together existing policies for conservation and to indicate the Department's intentions for future management. The Guide is presented in three sections. The first section explains the background to designation. The second section describes the special qualities of landscape, wildlife and heritage and the final section brings together

issues, policies and a programme for action to achieve the overall objectives for conservation of the area.

Designation of the Ring of Gullion AONB

THE RING OF GULLION IDENTITY

There are few small areas in Ireland which retain their local identity as clearly as the Ring of Gullion in South Armagh. At first sight this may seem strange for an area located astride the main routes north and south, almost midway between Belfast and Dublin, but on further inspection, the combination of the difficult hilly terrain and Ulster's ancient frontier, explains much of the distinctive culture and landscape.

The huge, heather clad, bulk of Slieve Gullion dominates the neatly divided countryside of walled fields and small farms of South Armagh. The mountain itself is encircled by the lower, rugged hills, known as the ring dyke, and between the mountain and its ring lie lowlands of

Foughill Otra and Slieve Gullion

varying width, from a narrow valley at Lislea to a broad plain at Killeen. The southern rim of the ring dyke is a natural boundary of Ulster, now the Border between Northern Ireland and the Republic of Ireland.

The Ring of Gullion has rich associations with Irish legends and myths. In the *Táin Bó Cuailgne* (the Cattle Raid of Cooley) Cuchulain is reputed to have defended Ulster, single-handed, against the hordes of Queen Maeve of Connacht — a battle traditionally associated with the Gap of the North. In another tale, Fionn Mac Cumhal was bewitched by Miluchra on the summit of Slieve Gullion at the Lough of Calliagh Bhirra.

Feelings about the landscape are expressed in local literature, folk history and art. The warm and welcoming people sit by hearths or in pubs singing songs, and recounting stories or poems featuring the days gone by, their neighbours and their homeland.

The Ring of Gullion has a distinctive landscape and it shares with the rest of South Armagh a unique cultural identity within Ireland. The landscape reflects not only the unusual physical structure of the rocks and the natural heath vegetation,

Farm at Milltown, Lislea

but also the way in which the land has been farmed and settled through thousands of years of occupation. Particularly attractive is the contrast of the rough, colourful mountain slopes of rock, heather, whin and bracken with the small, rectangular fields of lower slopes and valleys. Stone monuments and remains of buildings illustrate the story of the past and, with the small, traditional farmhouses with buildings grouped around a yard, they are parts of the rich, living heritage.

The Ring of Gullion has a clear physical identity. It is a special place and has long been thought so by local people. The make-up of the landscape, its history and its special features are the subject of Section 2 of this Guide. Section 3 contains preliminary policies and proposals for conserving the special landscape qualities and promoting their enjoyment.

CONSERVATION BACKGROUND

In the last forty years successive governments have endorsed policies for the conservation of special landscapes. Such policies applied in Britain and Ireland have led to a whole range of designations: National Parks, Areas of Outstanding Natural Beauty, Environmentally Sensitive Areas, Heritage Coasts, National Scenic Areas and other special designations such as the Norfolk Broads.

In Northern Ireland the Amenity Lands Act (Northern Ireland) 1965 made provision for the creation of both National Parks and Areas of Outstanding Natural Beauty (AONBs) but in fact only AONBs were designated. This early legislation aimed to protect the landscape merely by controlling development detrimental to the character of the areas designated. No provision was made for positive management or promotion of enjoyment.

The Nature Conservation and Amenity Lands (Northern Ireland) Order 1985 provided a new impetus for the management of countryside and scenic areas. The status given to Areas of Outstanding Natural Beauty was improved by the introduction of powers to make proposals for conservation. This has given

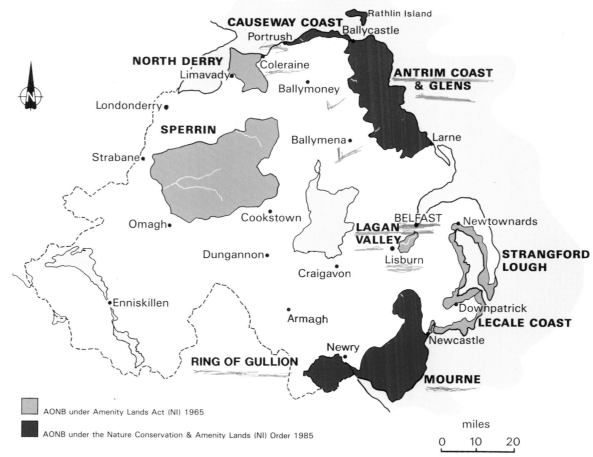

AONB under Amenity Lands Act (NI) 1965

AONB under the Nature Conservation & Amenity Lands (NI) Order 1985

miles
0 10 20

AONBs a more positive role and they are now considered to be a widely acceptable and appropriate designation for our prized scenic areas. Countryside and Wildlife Branch of the Environment Service of the Department of the Environment is the prime authority for the implementation of this new legislation.

Under the 1985 legislation three Areas of Outstanding Natural Beauty have been designated: Mourne AONB in 1986, Antrim Coast and Glens AONB in 1988 and Causeway Coast AONB in 1989.

Heather and bilberry

CONSULTATION

Before designation of the Ring of Gullion Area of Outstanding Natural Beauty all the consultations required under Article 14 of the Nature Conservation and Amenity Lands (Northern Ireland) Order 1985 were completed. Further steps were taken to consult the many organisations and members of the public with an interest in conservation.

On the boundary of the AONB Countryside and Wildlife Branch took the following consultative steps in order to reach a consensus opinion on the area considered worthy of designation:-

a. Early meetings with Newry and Mourne District Council.

b. Liaison with other branches of the Department of the Environment and with other government departments and bodies which have an interest in the resources and people of the area.

c. Consultation with the Council for Nature Conservation and the Countryside, the statutory advisory body to the Department of the Environment.

Gate at Lislea

d. Attendance at meetings with councillors of Newry and Mourne District Council. The council accepted the proposal to designate an AONB and made suggestions regarding the boundary.

e. In June 1989 a notice indicating the proposal to designate an AONB was placed in provincial and local newspapers and a map indicating the proposed boundary was displayed in community centres and libraries in the area. Leaflets were made freely available and representations were invited. Public meetings were arranged and staff from Countryside and Wildlife Branch, Historic Monuments and Buildings Branch and the Planning Service attended to answer queries.

f. All representations were considered by the Department. The inclusion of The Dorsey 'enclosure' was suggested in many responses and the District Council granted approval to this amendment to the boundary.

To determine policies and action points for this Guide to Designation, Countryside and Wildlife Branch consulted other branches within the Department of the Environment, other government departments, the District Council and a wide range of organisations having an interest in the area.

A BOUNDARY FOR THE RING OF GULLION AONB

The Ring of Gullion is defined topographically by the hills of the ring dyke. The boundary of the AONB generally includes these hills and their outer slopes, but a deviation to the west has been made to include the whole of a historic site, The Dorsey 'enclosure'. In the south the boundary lies along the Border with the Republic which, except in the Ravensdale area, coincides roughly with the ring dyke. In the west the AONB includes the valleys of the Cully Water and the Ummeracam River which separate the hills of the ring dyke from the rolling

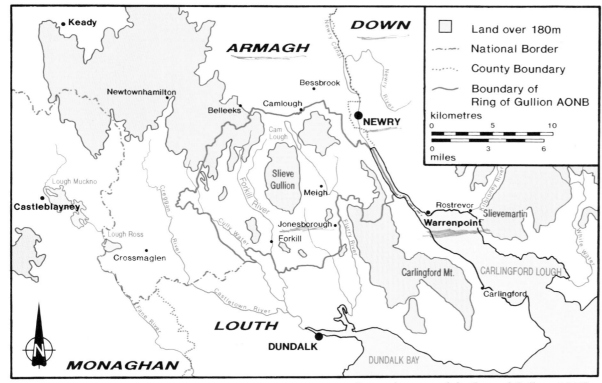

Regional setting of the Ring of Gullion AONB

View south from Mullaghbane Mountain

THE PURPOSE OF DESIGNATION

Designation of the Ring of Gullion AONB gives recognition to the national importance of its landscapes. However, designation must be accompanied by efforts to ensure the area retains its natural beauty and can be enjoyed by many. A wise and sustainable use of its resources should be encouraged and the environmental quality of the countryside should be enhanced where possible.

In the AONB proposals may be formulated for:

a. conserving or enhancing the natural beauty or amenities of the area;

b. conserving wildlife, historic objects or natural phenomena within it;

drumlin landscape extending towards Cullyhanna and Crossmaglen. In the north-west the ring dyke runs through the higher ground of The Fews where it is picked out by sharp rocky hills with a distinctive heath vegetation. The village of Camlough is not included, but the boundary then follows the Belfast-Dublin railway line to include the lower slopes of Camlough Mountain. Just south of the

quarry at Cloghoge it drops down to cross the Newry Canal and join the Newry River which then forms the boundary as far south as the Border at Fathom.

The AONB boundary line follows townland, road and field boundaries. The townland names are a record of the heritage of the area (Appendix 1). The total area is 15353 hectares.

c. promoting its enjoyment by the public;
   and

d. providing or maintaining public access
   to it.

Conservation tries to ensure that
development leads to sustained
environmental quality and long-term
benefits to the community. Conservation
does not necessarily oppose development.

The Countryside and Wildlife Branch of
the Environment Service, after a wide
consultation, has put together the relevant
policies of the different organisations with
interests and responsibilities in the Ring of
Gullion. These policies are the first step
towards a co-ordinated conservation
strategy for the AONB. A programme of
action to improve the conservation effort
and enhance public enjoyment has been
initiated. The Department will continue
to review the impact of these policies and
the effectiveness of the programme of
action.

An Outstanding Landscape

INTRODUCTION

The Ring of Gullion presents a striking landscape and the factors behind its appearance are complex. They embrace the fundamental geology, ecology and history of the area and their understanding is the key to the appreciation, conservation and enjoyment of this area of outstanding natural beauty.

Ring dyke hills

THE NATURAL HERITAGE

The distinctive landscape of the Ring of Gullion AONB owes much to long, complex and turbulent geological activity millions of years ago.

Like most of Counties Down and Armagh, the area has a base of Silurian shales and granite, but this comparative simplicity was later complicated by the eruption of volcanoes and the intrusion of lavas which together have caused the formation of the ring dyke and Slieve Gullion. Natural weathering processes over long periods of time, and significant erosion and deposition during the last Ice Age, added relief detail to this geologically complex area (Appendix 2).

Looked at from outside, the ring of rugged hills rises abruptly from surrounding lowland. The ring dyke hills, although steep and rocky, are narrow in width and, by a few narrow winding passes, one can gain entry into a remarkable secluded basin. A massive singular hill, Slieve Gullion, sits in the middle of the basin and in the background, some 6 miles distant, is another arc of the rugged hill-ring. The sense of enclosure becomes paramount.

Slopes of Slieve Gullion

The striking skyline summit of the ring dyke is punctuated by sharp peaks — Sturgan or Sugarloaf Hill, Slievenacappel, Mullaghbane Mountain, Slievebrack, Croslieve, Tievecrom, Slievebolea, Feede Mountain, Anglesey Mountain, Flagstaff, Fathom Mountain, Ballymacdermot Mountain and Camlough Mountain. The hard granite hills were glacially scoured leaving craggy outcrops, boulder strewn slopes, rocky ridges and hollows.

Slieve Gullion sits almost as a queen within her empire of the Ring and has in her wake a remarkable "tail" of boulder clay stretching south towards Drumintee. The mountain dominates over lowlands wrinkled by small streams or rivers moving quietly, generally south-easterly, through gently sloping or ill-drained lowland. The entrance or exit points for water or man are not obvious to the eye but narrow gaps in the ring dyke hills at Carrickcarnan, Kilnasaggart and Forkill provide important passes to the south.

Undoubtedly, Slieve Gullion and the ring dyke hills are the dominant features but the diversity of local landscape contributes much to the wealth and character of this Area of Outstanding Natural Beauty.

Cam Lough

In the north the major outlet is around Cam Lough where glaciers, some 20,000 years ago, formed a deep depression which later became flooded. Cam Lough, the largest lough in the area, is probably the best example of a glacial "ribbon" lake in Northern Ireland.

The western and eastern arcs of the ring dyke are broken at high levels and, from narrow winding roads circuiting the hills, there are striking views in many directions.

From Fathom Mountain and Flagstaff, on the eastern arc, there are outstanding views out over the Newry Canal, Newry River and Carlingford Lough to the Mourne Mountains and beyond. Turning round you can see the enclosed landscape with Slieve Gullion at its core. In the west of the Ring there are extensive views far east, west and south, as well as local valley and lakeland scenes with intricate detail in field, heath, trees and farmhouse.

People have lived in the Ring of Gullion for over 6,000 years and surviving today is a rich inheritance of historic monuments and many distinct features which have evolved with time. The area sits astride ancient and modern lines of communication and throughout history warfare and defence have been recurrent themes. The historic heritage paints a picture of the development of a distinct identity, as much part of the landscape as of the people.

The first clear evidence of human occupation in the Ring of Gullion comes from the age of the first farmers, the Neolithic. However, even earlier peoples, following a hunting and gathering economy, are known to have occupied sites on the coast at Dundalk Bay and may have travelled through the area in search of food. At that time much of the land would have been forested with native trees of oak, elm, hazel, alder, birch and pine.

The Neolithic farmers must have cleared trees from small plots to make way for tillage. A substantial and well-organised community would have been required to build the twenty or so large stone tombs which survive in the area. Many of these

Ballymacdermot Cairn

monuments are landmarks, sited in prominent positions, and views from them are magnificent, as at Ballymacdermot Cairn.

Three types of tombs are well represented. Court tombs have a semi-circular 'forecourt' bordered by a curving facade of upright stones which flank the entrance to the burial chambers. The King's Ring at Clontygora, the Black Castle at Annaghmare and the tomb at Ballymacdermot are some of the best examples of court tombs in the north of Ireland. A second type is the portal tomb, or dolmen, with a particularly fine example, the Hag's Chair, at Ballykeel. Here the chamber has been created by balancing a huge capstone on top of three upright stones. The third type is the passage tomb. These are large stone cairns in which a narrow passage leads to a

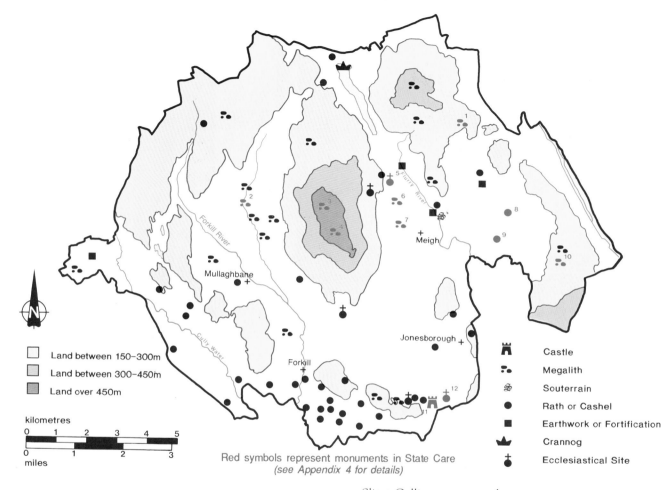

Land between 150-300m
Land between 300-450m
Land over 450m

kilometres
0 1 2 3 4 5

0 1 2 3
miles

Red symbols represent monuments in State Care
(see Appendix 4 for details)

Castle
Megalith
Souterrain
Rath or Cashel
Earthwork or Fortification
Crannog
Ecclesiastical Site

Excavations at several of these burial monuments have discovered human remains, pottery and stone tools. The evidence suggests that some sites continued in use for over a thousand years probably serving not only as burial sites but also as ceremonial focal points for the settled farming communities. No Neolithic house sites have been found in the area but the people probably lived in rectangular wooden houses.

Metal working arrived in the area about 4,000 years ago and the character of burials changed from large communal tombs to individual burials in small pits or stone cists, sometimes covered with a round cairn. Such a cairn, with two cists, survives on the northern summit of Slieve Gullion. A few standing stones, such as the Long Stone at Ballard, may also date from the Bronze Age.

The Iron Age, from about 250 BC to AD 400, is poorly represented in the archaeology of Ireland, though the earliest Irish sagas are believed to originate in these centuries. Dating from these apparently turbulent times is The Dorsey 'enclosure' located on the western edge of the Ring of Gullion. The Dorsey consists of the remains of two, roughly parallel, massive earth bank and ditch ramparts

broader burial chamber beneath the cairn. The finest tombs of this type are found in the Boyne Valley but the South Cairn on Slieve Gullion, although more modest, is a very dramatic site, commanding views over a huge area.

Slieve Gullion passage tomb

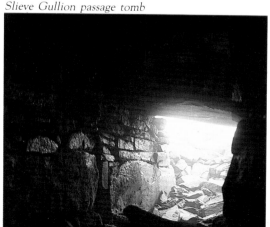

The Dorsey

over a mile long which lie astride an old routeway to *Eamhain Macha* (Navan Fort, near Armagh — the ancient capital of Ulster). Recent evidence gives it a date of about 100 BC, contemporary with a major phase of activity at Navan and so supporting the tradition that The Dorsey was then the 'gateway' of Ulster. Fragments of another similar earthwork known locally as The Dane's Cast survive at Aghayalloge near Meigh. These large scale linear earthworks appear to have been built as defensive features.

Christianity had arrived in Ireland by the 5th century and with it came the beginning of written records. There is also evidence for improvements in agriculture and many farming settlements survive from the Early Christian period (5th to 12th centuries AD). In the Ring of Gullion there are both ringforts with earth banks and ditches (raths) on the heavier soils, and with stone walls (cashels) on the rocky slopes of the ring dyke.

Good examples of cashels can be seen at Lisbanemore and Lisdoo (Killeen townland), at Lissacashel near Kilnasaggart and a memory persists in the name of Cashel townland. Raths are noticeably concentrated on south and south west slopes of the ring, particularly near Forkill in Carrickastickan and Tievecrom. At Lisleitrim near Cullyhanna, but outside the AONB, there is a spectacular hilltop rath with three substantial ditches and banks. The ancient settlement place-name element in old Irish 'lios' survives in many townland names.

Crannogs or island settlements are also features of Early Christian settlement in Ireland. A crannog in the north of Cam Lough was drowned when levels of the Lough were raised in the 19th century.

Throughout history routeways passing through the Ring have had an important influence on settlement. The *Slige Midluachra,* the ancient road from Drogheda to Dunseverick on the north coast of County Antrim, went through the Moyry Pass. Close to the road are two important religious sites, Kilnasaggart and

Kilnasaggart pillar stone

Killevy. The pillar stone at Kilnasaggart can be dated to about AD 700 and is the earliest dated cross-carved stone in Ireland. It marks the site of an Early Christian cemetery. Killevy, five miles to the north, is the site of one of Ireland's most important early convents founded by St Monenna (or Bline) in the 5th century.

Although plundered by the Vikings, monastic life continued here for a thousand years. The remains of two churches still stand but a round tower collapsed in the 18th century. The large, tree-lined graveyard is still in use and the nearby holy well, on the slopes of Slieve Gullion, continues to be venerated as a shrine to St Monenna.

Killevy Church

During the medieval period the Ring of Gullion was a troubled area on the edges of the English 'Pale' and lying across the main land routes north to castles at Newry, Downpatrick and Carrickfergus. Much of the land was clothed by either thick woods or inaccessible bogs, in marked contrast to the arable farms of the Norman manors in the lowlands of County Louth. The Ring of Gullion was traversed with difficulty, not least because of the independence and hostility of local chiefs.

In 1600, however, Lord Mountjoy secured the Moyry Pass, or Gap of the North, for the English. He built Moyry Castle on a natural rock hill which commands the pass. The castle, now in ruins, is a 3-storey tower with rounded corners and gun-loops. It was garrisoned by a constable and twelve men.

The Plantation of Ulster in the 17th century began to draw the borderland of South Armagh into a wider market economy. Pockets of British settlers established themselves on estates like those of Thomas Ball at Glassdrumman and Richard Jackson at Forkill. There was also an influx of Irish, seeking to win farmland from the uncultivated woods and bogs of the previously more inaccessible valleys and mountain slopes in the Ring of Gullion.

Moyry Castle

During the 18th century the major estate owners established new fairs or markets at Jonesborough, Forkill, Belleek and Camlough, linked to each other and the nearby towns by a network of new roads. The roads were essential to the improvement of agriculture, allowing both transport of materials, such as lime and turf, and the development of a market economy. The landscape was gradually transformed by the orderly creation of farm and field, market and road, according to the plans of the landlords and their agents.

Outside, but close to the Ring, the ports of Newry and Dundalk improved the opportunities for trade and, in particular, the growth of the local linen industry. The Newry Canal, opened in 1742, brought Newry to the forefront of Ulster's industrial revolution through the extensive hinterland of mid-Ulster, a position it retained well into the 19th century. The canal was succeeded by the Great Northern Railway, opened in 1852, and following the ancient route through the Gap of the North. The first power flax-spinning mill in Ireland was built just outside the AONB in Bessbrook, which subsequently became a prominent town with an estimated population of 3,500 in 1887. The lake at Camlough was enlarged and used to regulate the stream that supplied power to drive mills for grinding corn, scutching flax and bleaching linens. Although the linen industry was concentrated on the northern side of the mountains there were some scutch mills scattered within the Ring. Flax production and the linen industry provided an additional source of income to the small farmer, thus helping to sustain a high density of rural settlement.

By the mid-19th century the basic structure of the countryside, as we see it today, was in place. Bogs had been drained, mountain slopes brought into cultivation and farmhouses built down lanes or sited at intervals along the new, straight main roads. Only in a few locations did the irregular cluster of farm dwellings, known as clachans or streets, survive. These clachans, for example at Clontygora, Ballynamadda and Pollynagrasta, could have represented elements of the pre-Plantation settlement pattern and in general they were located alongside the older roads which followed spring lines along the lower hill slopes. Here farming communities could have benefited from rough pasture on the hills and cultivated land in the valley bottoms. In contrast, the large houses of the landlords set within wooded estates,

Killevy Castle

parkland and gardens represented the new features of the 19th-century landscape, for example, Heath Hall in Ballymacdermot townland and Killevy Castle. The historic buildings and their estates, though now mostly broken-up and neglected, are important in the present-day landscape.

The potato famine which struck in 1846-7 initiated a decline in the rural population and economy. In the Ring of Gullion death and emigration caused the loss of over a third of the population from townlands such as Edenappa, Foughill Etra and Foughill Otra. Today the ruins of farms, abandoned fields, derelict walls and overgrown lanes testify to the emigration from the countryside and changing economic circumstances.

MOUNTAIN, FIELD AND BOG

In the preceeding account we have seen how the natural landscape of the Ring of Gullion, the rocky mountains, native woods and bogs, have been transformed into productive farmland with scattered farms and small villages. In today's countryside, however, there is a variety of natural habitats modified to a greater or lesser extent by traditional and more modern agricultural practices and forestry.

Over a period of several thousand years following the last Ice Age, woodland had grown and matured into a complex community of woodland plants and animals, uninterrupted by human activity. Juniper, willow, birch, hazel and pine were prevalent on rocky hill slopes while alder, oak, ash, and elm were more typical of the better lowland soils. At the same time on water-logged sites bog moss accumulated, building up to form thick peat deposits and infill some of the small lake basins. As the bogs grew they further obstructed drainage and extended into surrounding woodlands. The preserved remains of trees can still be seen in many cutover bogs and the stumps of an ancient forest are visible where the peat has been cut back on the shores of Cashel Lough Upper.

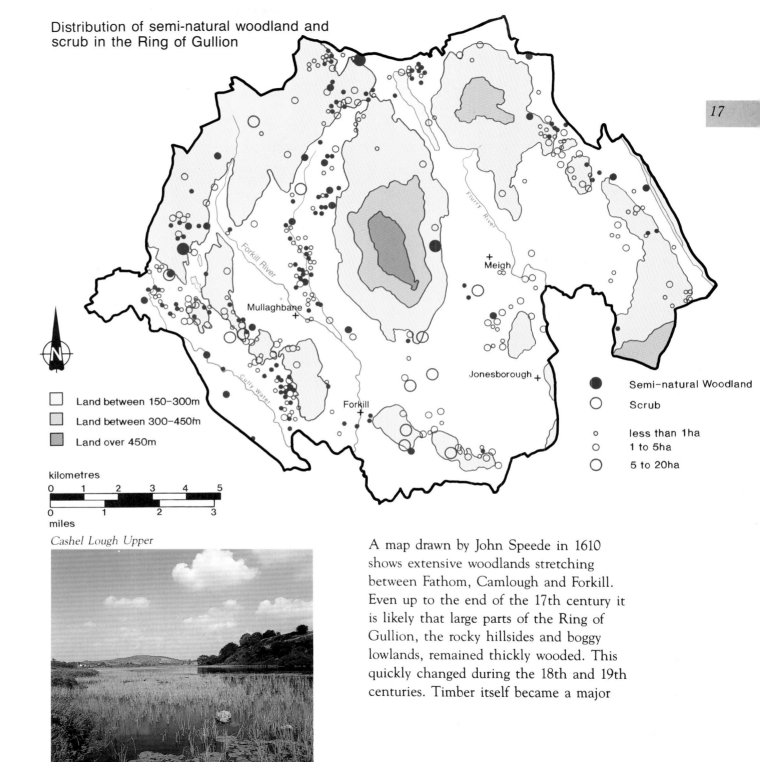

Distribution of semi-natural woodland and scrub in the Ring of Gullion

Land between 150–300m
Land between 300–450m
Land over 450m

kilometres
0 1 2 3 4 5

0 1 2 3
miles

Semi-natural Woodland
Scrub
less than 1ha
1 to 5ha
5 to 20ha

Cashel Lough Upper

A map drawn by John Speede in 1610 shows extensive woodlands stretching between Fathom, Camlough and Forkill. Even up to the end of the 17th century it is likely that large parts of the Ring of Gullion, the rocky hillsides and boggy lowlands, remained thickly wooded. This quickly changed during the 18th and 19th centuries. Timber itself became a major raw material, cleared land was converted for agriculture, the bogs were drained and turf was cut for fuel. Today by far the greatest proportion of trees are recent, coniferous plantations managed by the Forest Service. The native woodland cover is fragmentary and almost entirely of secondary origin, either planted or naturally regenerating scrub.

Scrub colonisation, Ummeracam

Private woodland, totalling about 150 hectares (370 acres), occurs in a variety of situations. On the steep slopes of valleys and hillsides small semi-natural woodlands of hazel and ash with sycamore, oak, rowan and willow are notable features. Willow, birch and alder scrub is typical of cutover peatland in the valley bottoms. The most mature woods are those which have been planted in old estates notably at Killevy Castle, Hawthorn Hill and Forkill.

In these plantations beech and oak are more common with a wide range of other planted trees including sycamore, elm, pine and larch. Groups of mixed trees are also a feature of many gardens, shelter belts around farms and in overgrown hedges. Beneath the trees the woodland ground flora includes plants which favour acidic soil conditions, usually dominated by bilberry, bracken and brambles.

Apart from woodland the other main natural habitats in the Ring of Gullion are heathland, bogs and small lakes. The craggy hills, with thin acidic soils overlying granitic rocks, have an extensive cover of heathland making up over a tenth of the AONB. The purples of heather, yellows of dwarf gorse, and oranges of bracken in the autumn, create rich mosiacs of colours which contrast markedly with the many greens which are the dominant hues of agricultural fields and hedges.

Heath at Ballard

Cotton grass on Camlough Mountain

The heaths themselves are very variable. Slieve Gullion is by far the largest area of heather moorland and consists of a fairly pure stand of ling, with scattered bilberry. Other areas around the lower hills of the ring dyke, as at Mullaghbane Mountain, Ummeracam and Ballard, have a much greater diversity of habitats and plants. Where the hard rocks have been scoured into a rock and ridge topography the areas of dry heath grade into flushes, fens and lakes. Dry heaths occur on freely-draining shallow peaty soils and are characterised by ling, bell heather and western gorse. Cross-leaved heath becomes more typical as peat becomes deeper and wetter, forming a wet heath community with deer grass, bog asphodel and cotton grass. Sedges and bog mosses are typical of the wet hollows and the margins of small loughs. Where heathland has been disturbed by over-grazing or repeated burning, bracken, gorse and bramble tend to be invasive.

The lowland bogs, so essential to rural life in the past, have been much disturbed by centuries of turf cutting, drainage and reclamation. Those that survive contain mixtures of bog mosses with drier banks of heather and bilberry often being colonised by willow or birch scrub.

Cam Lough is the largest body of water in the AONB and although its level was raised by the embankment built in the late 19th century it retains a lot of its natural character. The shoreline varies between steep rocky banks on the east and a gently shelving shore on the west. Along the

Cam Lough

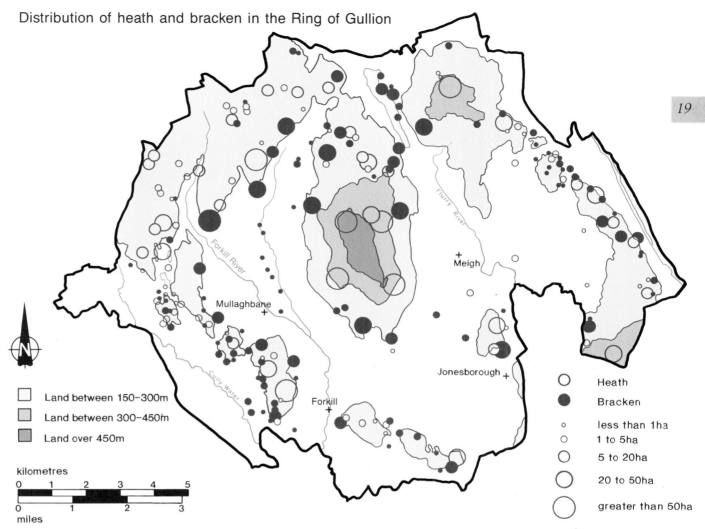

Land between 150–300m
Land between 300–450m
Land over 450m

kilometres
0 1 2 3 4 5

miles
0 1 2 3

○ Heath
● Bracken

∘ less than 1ha
○ 1 to 5ha
○ 5 to 20ha
○ 20 to 50ha
○ greater than 50ha

banks, marsh and scrub provide cover and nesting sites for many birds including mute swan, great crested grebes, moorhens, herons and warblers. The only other sizeable lakes in the area are Cashel Lough Upper and Lower. The Upper Lough is an attractive upland-type lake with clear, unpolluted water and containing water plants such as common reed, water horsetail and white water lily. The Lower Lough is surrounded by an extensive fringe of reed swamp and scrub woodland with alder and willow. Between and around the two loughs is a diverse area of rocky heathland and basin fens. Altogether the habitats provide excellent cover for wintering snipe and water rail.

The more productive farmland of the Ring has been improved progressively during the last few centuries. The best soils are those of the glacial deposits which run in rounded ridges through the lowlands between Slieve Gullion and its ring of hills. In these areas farmland is divided into strips of rectangular fields, each strip originally worked as one farm. The ditches dividing the fields usually comprise a combination of bank, stone wall and

Strip field pattern at Ballintemple

hedge in different proportions and varying from place to place. Stone walls are a particular feature around Aghadavoyle and Clontygora but hedges are more typical elsewhere.

In the past many farms would have grown some crops of oats and potatoes but now grassland and cattle dominate. Half of all farm businesses are classified as mainly beef cattle but sheep have become more important. (Appendix 3).

Marsh and butterfly orchids

The grassland has seen many years of intensive use and very few fields retain a natural diversity of plants, though some wet, flushed fields on the lower slopes of the mountains support species-rich grassland with marsh and butterfly orchids.

Forestry is also a major land use and it accounts for about 6% of the AONB. The broken topography of Slieve Gullion and

Camlough Forest

the ring dyke hills helps to accommodate forestry in the landscape. Forestry is of mixed coniferous species — mainly Sitka spruce, lodgepole pine, Japanese larch and Scots pine. The variety of species planted in irregular blocks with areas of unplanted hillside and pre-existing broad-leaved trees combine, in many cases, to produce attractive landscape features and pleasant areas for forest recreation.

Distinctive landscapes, such as the Ring of Gullion, are often the product of a distinctive cultural heritage, an intermingling of the people, their ways of life and the countryside, through history.

The people of the Ring of Gullion, in their virtually enclosed frontier position, share cultural traditions closely identified with their home territory. Such is the

natural complexity of the area that local areas within the Ring — Mullaghbane, Forkill, Jonesborough and Killeen — have their own particular characteristics of trade, tradition, folklore, poetry and language. Much can be attributed to the past difficulties in communication between

townland communities often separated by mountain, bog or stream. The independent community spirit, most clearly identified with the *ceilidh,* helped the people through difficult times by sharing labour, pooling resources and providing entertainment.

From late medieval times and probably earlier the whole of South Armagh was a notable centre of Irish poetry, and Creggan churchyard is famous as the burial place of poets. Although the use of English was increasing by the 18th century the area was still known as *Ceantar na n-Amhran* (The District of Songs) and also as *Ceantar na bh-Fill* (The District of Poets). The associated rich folk traditions of the Ring have been researched by T G F Patterson and Michael J Murphy. Today there is a marked revival of interest in the Irish language, folk singing and story telling.

Each locality and modern day village has its own individual history and landscape character.

In the east, **Cloghoge, Killeen, Clontygora** and **Fathom** have a special identity, perhaps influenced by their former isolation, by the intervening bogland from the remainder of the area.

Heather, gorse and bracken cover the upper slopes of Anglesey Mountain and the Fathom Hills, encroaching downslope on old pocket-sized fields with ruined walls. On lower slopes and on the valley

Farm lane, Clontygora

bottom the land is actively farmed within a neat pattern of rectangular or square fields bounded by tall, solidly constructed and well-maintained walls. Many wrought iron gates and square gate pillars of local character have been retained. Towards the valley bottoms the improved grasslands gradually give way to areas of cutover bog with an occasional willow bush. Trees occur in clusters of mature trees around old farmyards and scattered thorn bushes along field boundaries. There are some young conifer plantations on the slopes of Anglesey Mountain and on the outer, steep slopes of the Fathom hills a more

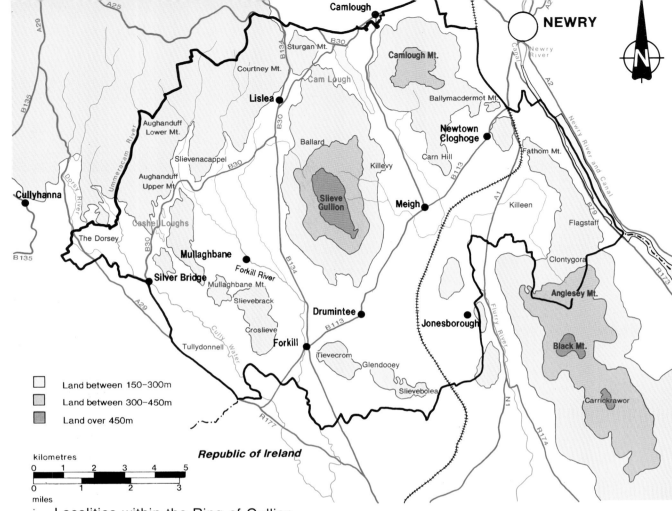

Localities within the Ring of Gullion

The hillslope and lowland landscapes around **Park View, Meigh, Drumintee** and **Jonesborough** have a complexity reflecting their position astride the main north-south routeways. There are remains of prehistoric graves and medieval churches and the more recent evidence of plantation estates, such as Heath Hall and Killevy Castle, make a significant landscape impact. Field size and patterns reflect local townland variations. Large

'Ladder' farm, Ballymacdermot

significant afforested area has been replanted with conifers. The entire area has a long settlement history with well-preserved ancient monuments including Clontygora Court Tomb (The King's Ring) and cashels at Lisbanemore and Lisdoo. From more recent times, on the lower slopes of Anglesey and Fathom Mountain, remnants of clachan communities remain standing amidst much new development. Elsewhere, farms and newer houses are dispersed along the main roads with many older buildings of local architectural interest. Green lanes and abandoned farmsteads are an indication of past settlement patterns and a much higher rural population.

fields are found adjacent to the old estates at Heath Hall and Killevy Castle but, on the hill slopes of Carn Hill and Cloghoge Mountain, the smaller fields and many houses were established by the native Irish labourers or small holders. On steeper slopes fields were arranged as 'ladder' farms. Field boundaries are mostly low stone walls or banks with overgrown shrubs — hawthorn, blackthorn, fuchsia and brambles. Mature trees and small areas of woodland are associated with the estates. The villages of Meigh, Drumintee and Jonesborough are highly visible in the open countryside. The lowland landscape can appear overcrowded by roadside settlement, but some balance is created by the rocky mountain slopes and the forestry on Slieve Gullion, Glendooey and Tievecrom. Everywhere there are signs of change with derelict farm buildings, abandoned estate houses, and new dwellings of varying design.

Around **Mullaghbane,** and west of Drumintee and Slieve Gullion, subtle landscape differences appear. Woodland, hedges, lakes and rocky slopes become more evident. The lowland is minutely subdivided into hedged fields and dominated by settlement dispersed alongside parallel road lines. There are remnants of bog with their birch and willow scrub. On slightly higher land west of Mullaghbane there are some larger farms and, in corners at the base of the steep ring dyke slopes, are a few small lakes. Croslieve (known locally as Creshla) has a very pronounced long scree slope and on the higher areas of Slievebrack, Tievecrom and Mullaghbane Mountain patches of woodland or forestry are broken by open hill and small, very rocky fields

becoming overgrown with bracken and gorse scrub. Traditional dwellings, many now abandoned, nestle into sheltered hillside pockets and are a valuable heritage of the area.

Outside the ring dyke and on the western perimeter of the AONB, the **Cully Water** valley is the dominant feature, with its meandering and often wooded river course. Farms are located in lines along the middle slopes, on either sides of the valley. Much of the land is improved grassland with thick thorn hedges, but on steeper valley sides and in the broken rocky ground around **Tullydonnell** there are patches of woodland and scrub. Further west there is a change of landscape character to the rolling drumlin countryside stretching away towards Crossmaglen. The Cully Water valley has been and is still an important routeway, with The Dorsey earthworks a key element in the heritage of the Ring of Gullion and the rest of Ulster.

Western slopes of Slieve Gullion

Cully Water

Further north around **Aughanduff, Annacloghmullin** and **Drumilly** the hills of the ring dyke run into the high ground of The Fews and the landscape lacks the rolling lowland element found elsewhere. Instead there are narrow valleys cut between small mountain blocks. It is an intricate landscape of small, enclosed rock basins, winding valleys and steep mountain slopes, around which the roads are obliged to bend or curve. Some land has been reclaimed for agriculture, the fields bounded by rough stone walls, earth banks and hedges, but steep and rocky slopes have an impenetrable mixture of scrub, woodland, whin, bracken and bramble.

Cashel Lough Upper

Cam Lough

Cashel Lough Upper and Lower lie in the centre of an extensive area of mixed heath, bog and wetland habitats. There are many derelict farms in the hills, but alongside the roads, at Davitt's Crossroads and Aughanduff, modernised and new two storey houses are the norm.

Some of the most dramatic landscapes in the AONB are found around **Cam Lough.** The lough occupies the bottom of the steep and narrow trough which separates Camlough Mountain from Slieve Gullion. The valley slopes plunge into the lough with only a rocky strip of shoreline. Although some remains of field boundaries are visible much of the hillsides are now

covered in bracken and brambles. The northern end of the lough opens out into a low-lying area of very broken and irregular topography, where some small fields surround rocky outcrops and boggy hollows. The north and east facing slopes of Camlough Mountain have a mixture of forestry, heath and 'ladder' farms. Being close to Camlough and Newry this north-eastern corner of the AONB has experienced a proliferation of new houses in the countryside.

Situated around the edge of the Ring of Gullion are the older villages of **Jonesborough, Forkill, Silverbridge** and **Camlough.** They were established by the local landlords in the 18th century as market centres on the main lines of communication. The other settlements in the area — **Meigh, Mullaghbane, Drumintee** and **Lislea** — are all located in townlands of the same name in the lowlands surrounding Slieve Gullion. Each is essentially a crossroads settlement with one or more churches, a school, post office, shop and a pub. Elsewhere the settlement is sited close to the roads or loosely clustered.

Forkill's location in the narrow gap between the ring dyke mountains of Croslieve and Tievecrom was significant in its development as an important market centre in the mid-18th century. In 1888 it was described in George Bassett's *Survey of Armagh* as an industrial village with a corn mill, scutch mill, hotel, post office, and several grocery and drapery shops.

Forkill village

Just up the road is **Mullaghbane** with its attractive setting in the broad valley between Slieve Gullion and the ring dyke hills. Mullaghbane was closely associated with the local landlord Richard Jackson who built a Rectory there in 1767. In the mid 19th century the village contained little more than the Roman Catholic Church, a National School and

schoolmaster's house. A Church of Ireland church was built by the side of the road between Mullaghbane and Forkill but the building is no longer in use.

Jonesborough has its origins in the early 18th century, founded by an English soldier, Colonel Morris Jones. His residence on top of Jonesborough's hill still exists, as does the row of cottages he built in the village. The Flurry River, the county boundary, divided the village into two separate settlements known as Jonesborough and Flurrybridge. The old Belfast to Dublin mail coach stopped at the sub-post office at Flurrybridge. Today Jonesborough is a linear village bisected by the Border lying along the Flurry River. The Sunday market, which began in 1974, has become well established and Jonesborough has developed as a small commercial centre.

Meigh, situated on the valley floor between Slieve Gullion and Fathom Mountain, is a small, relatively recent, crossroads village providing a service centre for the Killevy area.

Drumintee and **Lislea** are both closely associated with the church. The Roman Catholic Church at Drumintee was built in 1870 on the prominent glacial 'tail' of

Slieve Gullion. The church at Lislea is earlier (1822) but both have provided a stimulus to the more recent growth of the settlements.

Drumintee Church

Camlough village is situated along the Newtownhamilton to Newry Road on the north side of the AONB. In the early 19th century several flax and corn mills were built beside the Camlough River providing local employment. The market tradition established in the 18th century continues today with a busy livestock market. The village is now an important residential and commercial centre on the outskirts of Newry.

In recent years settlements within the AONB have generally experienced a degree of expansion with the growth of housing estates and community facilities. There has also been considerable development of new individual dwellings in the countryside. Mobility, provided by cars, has allowed a measure of re-vitalisation, as people can travel further to work and yet continue to live locally in a village or the countryside. New development and dereliction are perhaps different sides of the same coin but each new development has its impact on the landscape and each derelict house is a loss of heritage.

Glendesha

Conservation and Development

INTRODUCTION

The Ring of Gullion is an outstanding landscape. The geologically unique ring of hills has produced an almost secret hiding place in which people have developed particular ways of life and strong community ties. It has many distinctive landscape features in the patterns of fields and settlement with the hedges or walls, gates and traditional buildings. There is a remarkable concentration of historic monuments and a variety of natural vegetation important for wildlife. All these qualities should be cherished and protected so that they can be enjoyed today and into the foreseeable future. Their conservation will require active protection and the channelling of development in such a way as to produce long term environmental benefits, adding to rather than detracting from, the wealth of heritage.

This Section states the broad objectives, backed up by more specific policies, which will underlie the activities of public bodies relating to the AONB. In addition, proposals for action indicate the commitment agreed by the relevant government departments, District Council and other organisations (see Appendix 5 for abbreviations used in this Section). Altogether this should bring real benefits

to the community and countryside over a period of about five years, after which policies and action proposals may be usefully reviewed.

Significant results will not be achieved unless the departments and public bodies work together. Local community associations and landowners are also of crucial importance as the countryside of the AONB is largely in private ownership. Management of privately owned land will continue to be in the hands of individual farmers and landowners but, as in the past, some of their decisions will be influenced by government policy. Some land, such as the forests, and some facilities, such as roads or picnic sites, are in public

ownership and are managed directly by the government. The policy statements and proposals for action presented in this document are the first step towards co-ordinated countryside management within the AONB. An arrangement for reviewing future policies and proposals must be established in consultation with the District Council and the relevant government departments and agencies.

Farming is a major activity in the AONB and there are some 500 farm businesses. Use of the land for agriculture has shaped the landscape of farm, field and mountain as we see it today and it is the husbandry of farmers which will maintain or determine the appearance of the countryside for future generations.

Tamnaghbane

Small farms predominate with an average farm holding of 15 hectares (38 acres) and only 16 farms with more than 50 hectares (125 acres). Three-quarters of the farm businesses are classified as very small and additional sources of income are required to maintain and improve living standards. Opportunities for diversification have been limited, though mushroom growing has met with some success.

Farm improvement and rationalisation have occurred, but at some environmental cost through the removal of field boundaries, the reclamation of heath or bog and the building of intrusive modern farm sheds. On the other hand, on smaller and marginal farm holdings, particularly on the southern edge of the ring dyke, reduced farming intensity and abandonment are evident with the spread of bracken and gorse. Traditional field boundaries — hedges, banks, walls and ditches — are often unmanaged or overgrown. Replacement of traditional boundaries and gates with post and wire fences, concrete pillars and tubular steel gates is causing a gradual erosion of landscape quality. With reduced government and European Community support for agricultural production, the trend towards a lower level of agricultural activity appears likely to continue. However, the changing farm economy creates an opportunity to ensure that any new measures which are introduced are beneficial, in the widest sense, to the well-being of the countryside.

- to encourage support for an active farming community;

- to encourage farmers to respect and care for the wildlife, landscape and archaeological interests of their farms;

- to ensure that conservation and enhancement of the environment become an integral part of all farming activity;

- to provide advice and grant-aid to farmers wishing to undertake conservation projects or to provide facilities for enjoyment of the countryside; and

- to direct appropriate resources to research and development, advice and education in pursuit of environmentally friendly farming.

3.1.3   ACTION

- to improve co-operation between advisory services to provide local guidance on pollution control and appropriate farm conservation measures (Action: DANI, EPD, CWB, CVNI, FWAG(NI));

- to improve information on sources of grant aid (Action: DANI, CWB, UFU, NIAPA, RDC);

- to encourage the management of hedges, gates and walls of historic or wildlife value (Action: CWB, DANI);

- to encourage farmers to plant mixed native trees particularly around farm buildings and in small areas not easily managed for other purposes (Action: CWB, DANI); and

- to assess the need for support measures for environmentally sensitive farming specific to the Ring of Gullion or for designation as an Environmentally Sensitive Area (Action: DANI, CWB, HMBB).

Gate at Tievecrom

3.2   FORESTRY

3.2.1   ISSUES

Forestry accounts for 990 ha (6.4%) of the AONB. It is an important land use and makes a significant landscape impact. All the larger plantations are owned or managed by DANI Forest Service. Their ownership includes extensive unplanted areas of Slieve Gullion which are managed for wildlife and recreation.

The broken nature of the topography on the hills, the irregular pattern of land holdings and the varied species composition have helped to integrate forests into the landscape and provide a variety of wildlife habitats. Some straight plantation edges remain discordant and there are internal boundaries which run against the grain of the countryside. Small isolated blocks of forestry can also appear obtrusive. As the plantations mature increasing areas will be felled and replanted, as at Fathom Forest, and at this stage opportunities are taken for improving forest design, enhancing landscape and promoting wildlife interest. In addition to operating a commercial forestry enterprise, DANI Forest Service also provide recreational facilities at Slieve Gullion and Camlough Forests (see Section 3.12). All

Camlough Forest

aspects of forest management can be discussed at the Down and Armagh Forest District Conservation Committee. Any significant afforestation within the AONB would be subject to the Environmental Assessment (Afforestation) Regulations (NI) 1989.

Edge of plantation

- to ensure that new forest planting and management of existing forests give due regard to landscape, wildlife and historic interests;

- to encourage increased planting of native broad-leaved trees in both State-owned and private planting schemes;

- to ensure the integrated use of forests for conservation, recreation and education as well as timber production; and

- to improve forest recreation facilities so that they are complementary to other facilities in the AONB and surrounding countryside.

3.2.3   ACTION

- to consult with appropriate bodies on all planting, felling and replanting proposals within State-owned forests (Action: DANI(FS), CWB, HMBB);

- to prepare management plans for Forest Nature Reserves and unplanted areas of State-owned forests (Action: DANI(FS));

- to develop and promote walking, and other passive recreational activities on Forest Service land (Action: DANI(FS), NMDC);

- to discourage dumping by the public on Forest Service land (Action: DANI(FS), NMDC); and

Walled garden, Slieve Gullion Forest Park

3.3 WOODLAND AND TREES

3.3.1 ISSUES

Within the Ring of Gullion trees and small woods are significant landscape features and valuable wildlife habitats. In the farmed countryside small groups of trees in shelter belts or hedges provide beneficial shelter for stock and help to screen farm buildings.

Native woodland had been largely cleared from the area during the 18th century. What remains is generally on small areas of steep hillside, in valleys or on bogs where woodland has regenerated. Planted broad-leaved woods and parklands are found around estate houses, farms and church buildings and they have a strong influence on the landscape. Trees also occur in hedges or along streams. In some areas, such as around Meigh and Newtown Cloghoge, buildings tend to be obtrusive because of the lack of trees.

A survey of woodland carried out for the Department* found that most of the woodlands are unmanaged and their nature conservation value has been reduced by livestock grazing, dumping of litter and invasion by sycamore.

Park and woodland at Hawthorn Hill

Grants for woodland, tree planting and management are available from DANI but there has been only a very limited uptake in the area. However, a welcome initiative by local parishes has seen many churchyards planted with broad-leaved trees in the last few years. Newry and Mourne District Council has also encouraged the care of an important group of trees near Forkill by incorporating them in a local amenity scheme.

**Tree Survey of South Armagh
Queen's University of Belfast, 1987*

3.3.2 POLICIES

- to foster the nature conservation value of woods and trees;

- to encourage the management of existing woodland, hedges and trees and support new planting of native or locally traditional trees;

- to consider the use of Tree Preservation Orders to protect trees or woodland of special amenity value which are under threat and which are not overmature; and

- to encourage the use of trees in environmental improvement schemes.

Rowan tree

- to encourage tree planting under grant schemes (Action: DANI(FS), CWB);

- to provide a new grant for landowners or community groups to encourage native tree planting in appropriate small areas not eligible for existing grants (Action: CWB);

- to attach conditions to planning consents for new housing or commercial developments requiring the retention of existing trees, and new planting in appropriate cases (Action: TCPS, CWB);

- to publish a leaflet giving information about the local character of woods and trees and advice on woodland management and tree planting (Action: DANI(FS), CWB, HMBB); and

- to protect and improve the most important woods, eg in graveyards and old estates, using grants or management agreements with landowners where appropriate (Action: CWB, DANI(FS), CVNI).

Trees in churchyard at Forkill

3.4 RIVERS, CANALS AND LOUGHS

3.4.1 ISSUES

The Ring of Gullion contains a number of small rivers and several loughs. In the boggy valley bottoms sheughs have been cut to improve drainage. Each of these watercourses is an important wildlife habitat and landscape feature, and some are used for water supply. All are vulnerable to accidental pollution from farm or domestic sources. The Newry Ship Canal and Cam Lough support good coarse fisheries with roach, bream, rudd, eels and pike.

Cam Lough is a multi-purpose water resource which was at one time considered for use in a pump-storage hydroelectric power scheme. The lough is an important resource in the current and future public water supply strategy and will be used in increasing quantities to cater for growing demand. The lough is also becoming popular for a variety of recreation activities and Newry and Mourne District Council has provided car parks and picnicing facilities in two areas alongside the lough. The variety of interest suggests that an integrated management strategy is required.

Victoria Lock, Newry Ship Canal

Cashel Lough Upper and Lower are important wildlife habitats and merit special attention.

The Newry Ship Canal is a major feature on the eastern edge of the AONB. Not only has it been a very important navigation route into Newry port and the canal network within Ulster but it has an attractive natural woodland fringe.

White water lilies

- to retain, and enhance where possible, the quality of freshwater and riverine environments;

- to manage water supply reservoirs and catchments to safeguard water resources;

- to monitor and regulate effluent disposal from industry, waste disposal sites and sewage treatment works;

- to pursue vigorously a reduction of farm source pollution through advice, research and grant-aid to farmers;

- to ensure that drainage schemes, channel maintenance and fishery developments do not impair the riverside environment and water regime; and

- to support the development of the Newry Ship Canal for recreation and conservation.

- to prepare a management plan for Cam Lough taking into account its growing importance as a water resource and its special wildlife, recreation and historic interests (Action: CWB, HMBB, EPD, WS, NMDC, NIE);

- to conduct river corridor landscape and wildlife surveys prior to drainage works on all watercourses (Action: DANI); and

- to support the establishment of a Newry Canal Wildlife Refuge (Action: NMDC, CWB).

Heron in Forkill River

Within its small area the Ring of Gullion has a wide range of wildlife habitats extending from the tidal mudflats of the Newry River to the eroded blanket bog on the summit of Slieve Gullion, over 500m above sea level. The most extensive semi-natural vegetation is the heathland which covers Slieve Gullion and the peaks of the ring dyke hills, making up over 12% of the area. Much of the lower altitude heathland supports a diverse plant and insect community associated with the mosaic of small pools, bogs, wet grassland and heather.

Heathland is maintained by judicious grazing and burning. Too much grazing can convert heather to coarse grasses. Too little grazing, especially in areas previously heavily grazed or burnt, can allow the spread of bracken, gorse and brambles. Significant areas of the AONB are already dominated by bracken (4%) and gorse scrub (3%).

Heath and bog, Slieve Gullion

Only small fragments remain of the once extensive lowland bogs in the valley bottoms. These areas of abandoned cutover bog contain deep pools, banks of bilberry and heather and a regenerating cover of birch and willow scrub.

Most of these natural habitats lie on the margins of more intensively farmed land and provide limited rough grazing. Their

conservation is clearly dependent on continuing, environmentally sensitive farm practices.

Other aspects of wildlife conservation are covered under the headings agriculture (3.1), forestry (3.2), woodland (3.3) and canals, rivers and loughs (3.4).

3.5.2 POLICIES

● to conserve and enhance wildlife habitats; and

● to protect rare and endangered species.

3.5.3 ACTION

● to survey the lakes, fens and lowland heaths of the area and identify the highest quality sites (Action: CWB);

● to conserve and enhance the highest quality sites through ASSI declaration (see Appendix 6), management agreements, and payments to landowners, where appropriate (Action: CWB);

● to provide advice and information about the wildlife of the area and to encourage projects which aim to conserve or promote understanding of wildlife eg nature trails and guides (Action: CWB); and

● to conduct a baseline survey of land use and wildlife habitats, and to monitor future changes (Action CWB).

Common Hawker

West door, Killevy church

The Ring of Gullion has a distinctive and well-preserved heritage. It embraces legends, folklore and Irish literature, as well as historic monuments, routeways, traditional farm buildings and landscape features. Several historians and historical societies are active in the area.

Twelve of the best preserved and more important sites are protected in State Care and nine of these are managed by the Department's Historic Monuments and Buildings Branch (Appendix 4). An additional 23 sites, on private land, are protected as scheduled ancient monuments. Although local people have a high degree of respect for ancient monuments, sites can still be damaged by accident, ignorance or neglect. Public enjoyment of this heritage is encouraged at State Care sites through provision of signposts, access and explanatory notices. Interesting sites on private land, on the other hand, are not freely accessible to the general public.

Most buildings of historical interest — farms, mills, rectories, and old estate houses and outbuildings — are in private ownership. Many of the small traditional single-storey farmhouses are now derelict, some abandoned and others replaced by modern houses. There is a danger, if current trends persist, that much of the distinctive character of small farm houses, yards and gates will gradually disappear.

Whilst the heritage of the Ring of Gullion, and South Armagh in general, is well known by local people there is scope for extending its appreciation among the wider public.

Clontygora court cairn

- to foster the already strong community interest and involvement in the cultural heritage and assist in the publication of information, guides and educational material;

- to protect and conserve historic monuments and buildings;

- to advise farmers and other landowners on the care and protection of historic features and archaeological sites; and

- to encourage continued use, maintenance and renovation of traditional buildings.

Listed building at Aghadavoyle

- to publish a detailed archaeological survey (Action: HMBB);

- to continue to protect all scheduled historic monuments and to schedule other important monuments (Action: HMBB);

- to promote the archaeology and history of the area by provision of heritage trails, leaflets, signposts and access arrangements (Action: HMBB, CWB, RS, NMDC and local historical societies);

- to support Newry and Mourne District Council, community groups and historical societies in their sensitive care or restoration of areas and buildings of interest (Action: HMBB, CWB);

- to endeavour to agree arrangements for access to and interpretation of The Dorsey earthworks (Action: HMBB, NMDC, CWB);

- to commission a survey of industrial archaeology to identify sites of interest and make suggestions for their conservation and promotion (Action: HMBB, CWB);

- to commission a survey of traditional buildings to determine the location, siting and design characteristics of such buildings and prepare guidelines for their maintenance and renovation (Action: CWB, HMBB, TCPS);

- to complete the survey and listing of historic buildings (Action: HMBB); and

- to support the repair and maintenance of listed historic buildings by means of advice and grant aid (Action: HMBB).

3.7 NEW DEVELOPMENT

3.7.1 ISSUES

Dispersed rural settlement is the traditional pattern of the area. The settlement pattern has however been changing with new roadside dwellings built to replace older, sub-standard houses which are often situated down lanes. The materials used and the new building designs often show little affinity with older houses, and the treatment of adjoining gardens and boundaries contrasts markedly with surrounding fields, walls and hedges. Sited in more prominent positions they could be one of the greatest threats to the outstanding landscape quality. In the words of Estyn Evans in his book *Mourne Country*:-

"It is the new house by the roadside that takes the eye, not the low whitewashed homestead sheltering under a ring of wind blown trees."

People living in rural areas generally help to maintain the vitality of community life but there should be a much greater appreciation of the impacts of rural housing in the countryside.

Within the AONB the villages are small but they are important local service centres for the dispersed rural population. They have housing estates, individual houses and community and commercial developments. Each village will continue to be a focus for the community. Environmental improvements to enhance the quality of life can soften their visual impact on the surrounding countryside.

Meigh

The Department's Town and Country Planning Service has recently prepared a Rural Subject Plan for the area in full consultation with all concerned parties. The Plan has been adopted following a Public Enquiry in 1989. Standards for location, siting and design of new development in rural areas throughout Northern Ireland were published in 1987. Regulations, published in 1989, require an environmental statement where proposed development is likely to have significant effects on the environment by virtue of factors such as its nature, size or location. Guidelines for the design and siting of agricultural buildings are given in the booklet *The Siting and Design of Farm Buildings in the Countryside* published by DANI.

New rural housing

- to recognise the positive role of villages through their promotion as residential, service and, where appropriate, tourist centres;

- to encourage commercial development in villages provided the scale of development is suited to the setting;

- to promote the infilling of street frontages, the conservation of street character, the reuse of derelict land, and the planting of trees to improve the appearance of villages;

- to require new buildings in the countryside to respect and reflect the traditional styles and settlement pattern of the locality. A high standard of design of all new buildings will be required;

Renovated farmhouse

- to encourage the retention or reconstruction of traditional boundary details such as hedges, walls, trees and gates around all new development;

- to restrict inappropriate development in areas of high landscape quality; and

- to discourage destruction or damage of valuable heritage sites and important wildlife habitats.

- to survey traditional buildings and evaluate the effects of planning policies in the past in order to prepare a location, siting and design guide for new development in the AONB (Action: CWB, TCPS, HMBB);

- to promote the protection of gates and other traditional features on farms and encourage all agricultural building work to be carried out sensitively, with consideration given to its effects on the landscape and the countryside (Action: DANI); and

- to promote tidying and tree planting at key villages (Action: NMDC, CWB, NIHE, voluntary bodies and local community associations).

Types of gates

3.8   MINERAL EXTRACTION

3.8.1   ISSUES

Forkill has the only working quarry within the AONB. Several other sites are disused. The principal mineral resource is the Newry granite used for roadstone. By their nature mineral operations have the potential to cause considerable environmental damage, including visual degradation of the landscape and pollution. The Department's policies on mineral extraction are stated in detail in the Newry and Mourne Rural Area Subject Plan 1986-1999.

3.8.2   POLICIES

- to safeguard the scenic beauty, wildlife habitats and historic features of the AONB through rigorous control of mineral developments; and

- if any permissions are granted for mineral development, to exercise stringent controls over operations and site restoration by the stipulation of conditions to minimise any harmful effects on the landscape.

3.9   WASTE DISPOSAL AND LITTER

3.9.1   ISSUES

Enjoyment of the Ring of Gullion countryside can easily be spoilt by litter, tipping and pollution. Illegal tipping of domestic and building waste on roadside sites and careless disposal of litter at informal picnic sites are particular problems. Car dismantling is an important local business but can also be an eyesore and source of pollutants.

3.9.2   POLICIES

- to protect the environment from degradation and pollution by the incorrect disposal of waste materials;

- to encourage the provision of civic amenity sites or special collection services;

- to ensure that waste disposal sites and scrapyards are located, used and reinstated with due respect for environmental health, pollution, landscape, wildlife and heritage considerations; and

- to encourage appropriate screening around waste disposal sites, civic amenity sites and scrapyards.

3.9.3   ACTION

- to encourage an initial clean-up campaign (Action: CVNI, NMDC and local community groups);

- to facilitate local initiatives to increase litter awareness and stimulate anti-litter or re-cycling activities (Action: NMDC, EPD, NI 2000, TNI and local community groups);

- to promote anti-litter education in schools (Action: CWB, EPD, SELB); and

- to introduce legislation which will effectively address the problems of litter and illegal dumping of waste (Action: EPD).

3.10   COMMUNICATIONS

3.10.1   ISSUES

Apart from the main A1 Belfast-Dublin trunk road the area is characterised by a network of minor roads. Most roads date from the 18th and 19th centuries and have been modified and improved over the years. Stone banks, overgrown thorn hedges, drystone ditches and, in places, avenues of beech trees are attractive roadside features. Roadside verges and hedges are important wildlife habitats. However, narrow carriageways with sharp bends and poor visibility at junctions are hazards to traffic on the more heavily used routes, in particular the Newry to Crossmaglen and Newtownhamilton roads. The proposed Newry by-pass, Phase 3, lies along the eastern edge of AONB.

The area is also traversed by the Great Northern Railway, Belfast to Dublin line. The line of the disused Dundalk, Newry and Greenore Railway lies along the foot of Fathom Mountain beside the Omeath Road.

The Newry Ship Canal, between Newry and Victoria locks is currently being

Road verge at Drumintee

restored by Newry and Mourne District Council, the refurbishment of the Victoria Locks being completed in June 1991.

Historically and to the present day, the Ring of Gullion has been a border area traversed by major lines of communication. Though many people pass through the area by road or rail, few stop to appreciate its natural beauty and heritage.

- to continue to develop, manage and maintain a safe and convenient road network;

- to ensure that any road improvement scheme is sensitive to the local landscape character, retaining or replacing traditional hedges or walls wherever appropriate;

- to manage roadside, canal and railway verges for the benefit of wildlife;

- to encourage the planting of locally traditional tree and shrub species within road boundaries, where appropriate; and

- to improve the opportunities for road users to enjoy the countryside.

- to make progressive, environmentally sensitive, improvements to the Newry to Crossmaglen road and other roads carrying a high volume of traffic in the AONB (Action: RS, CWB);

- to encourage signposting and footpaths to appropriate areas or sites of landscape, wildlife or historic interest by the provision or retention of green lanes, stiles and traditional farm gates (Action: CWB, HMBB, NMDC); and

- to restore the Newry Ship Canal and provide public access along the towpath (Action: NMDC, CWB).

Newry Ship Canal

3.11 MILITARY ESTABLISHMENTS

Within the AONB there is a border check point on the A1 south of Newry and several military observation posts on prominent hills of the ring dyke. These establishments are unsightly and can deter public access. They damage any popular image of South Armagh.

- to improve the image of South Armagh as an attractive area with opportunities for countryside recreation;

- to minimise, as far as circumstances permit, the impact of military installations on public enjoyment of the Ring of Gullion; and

- to ensure that the security forces are informed of the location of historic monuments and sites of special wildlife interest.

3.12 ENJOYMENT OF THE COUNTRYSIDE

3.12.1 ISSUES

The countryside of the Ring of Gullion provides many opportunities for informal recreation and leisure activities. These include picnicing and scenic drives, walking or rambling, cycling, horse riding, fishing and shooting, to mention but a few. A number of viewpoints and picnic sites, for example at Flagstaff and Cam Lough, are provided by the District Council. Forest Service maintains a scenic drive, walks and picnic sites in Slieve Gullion Forest Park and walks in Camlough Forest. Historic monuments in State Care are accessible to the public and elsewhere access to the wider countryside is informal and along roads, old farm lanes and tracks.

The existing facilities are used mostly by local people and there is considerable scope for encouraging a greater level of participation from outside the area in countryside recreation. Tourism (involving overnight accommodation) is currently a minor feature, with at present only five guest houses offering bed and breakfast accommodation. There are no hotels or roadside cafes/restaurants within the area.

Recreation at Cam Lough

Enjoyment of the countryside can be strengthened by the availability of information to assist in appreciation and create greater understanding. Such information includes signposts and notices, displays, leaflets and interpretation centres or museums. Interpretation is at present available at Slieve Gullion Forest Park and Mullaghbane Folk Museum. Explanatory notices are located at some historic monuments. Newry Arts Centre and other community centres are well positioned to help promote the enjoyment of the area.

A variety of publications, for example the journal of The Creggan Local History Society, help to communicate the very special character of the area.

Ballintemple viewpoint

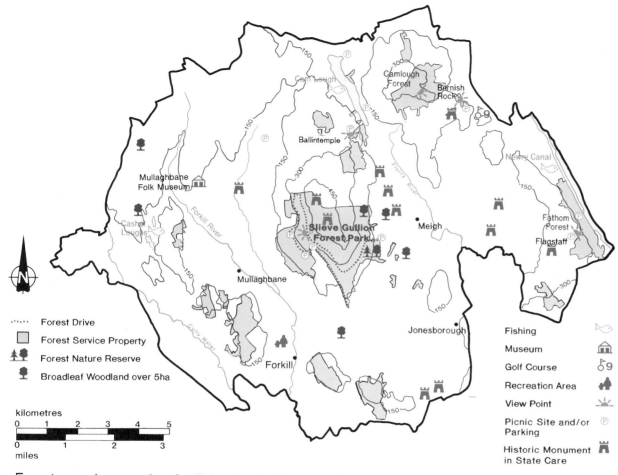

Legend

..... Forest Drive

▢ Forest Service Property

🌲 Forest Nature Reserve

🌳 Broadleaf Woodland over 5ha

kilometres

```
0    1    2    3    4    5
```

```
0         1         2         3
miles
```

Fishing	🐟
Museum	🏛
Golf Course	⛳
Recreation Area	🏕
View Point	🌅
Picnic Site and/or Parking	Ⓟ
Historic Monument in State Care	🏰

Forestry and recreation facilities in the Ring of Gullion

The scenic countryside with its rich heritage and opportunities for recreation provides a basis for further development. A Tourism Appraisal of South Armagh is currently being carried out by a group known as Regeneration of South Armagh (ROSA) in conjunction with Newry and Mourne District Council and a marketing strategy is being prepared jointly for Newry and Mourne, and Down District Councils. Cross Border initiatives are also being given consideration by the Irish Border Regions Association. AONB designation adds to the status of the Ring of Gullion area in any tourism strategy.

- to advise, encourage and assist with grant-aid, where appropriate, the District Council and other bodies or individuals in the provision of facilities for enjoyment of the countryside, eg picnic sites, footpaths, nature trails and public open space;

- to seek to minimise the risk of damage to or trespass on private property and sensitive sites of historic or wildlife interest; and

- to advise on and co-operate in the provision of information and interpretative material about the landscape, wildlife, heritage and enjoyment of the AONB.

Walking in Slieve Gullion Forest

- to appoint a Countryside Officer with responsibility on the ground to initiate projects and co-ordinate activities of various organisations within the AONB (Action: CWB); and

- to establish a management group to prepare a co-ordinated recreation strategy for the AONB. The strategy might include for example:-

— development of Slieve Gullion Forest Park as a focus for the area;

— a management plan for Cam Lough;

— an open farm with heritage, wildlife and educational interests;

— nature reserves with public access;

— an educational centre and youth hostel;

— a network of facilities and routes for waymarked footpaths and bridleways;

— restocking of Newry Ship Canal and lakes for fishing;

— development of Newry Ship Canal for recreation;

— theme trails (eg heritage and geology);

— car parks at Mullaghbane Folk Museum and Cashel Lough;

— an interpretation/heritage centre;

— a range of accommodation including restoration of traditional farmhouses as self-catering units;

— tourist information and promotional literature;

— roadside signing and information about the AONB; and

— publication of guidebooks, leaflets and route cards.

(Action: NMDC, CWB, HMBB, DANI(FS), WS, NITB, SCNI, RS, SELB and local community groups).

3.13   RURAL DEVELOPMENT

South Armagh, including the Ring of Gullion, is an area of high unemployment and declining agriculture (Rural Action Project 1987). Traditionally, part-time farming was combined with seasonal work in nearby towns, or across the water.

Mullaghbane Folk Museum

These opportunities for combining farming with other employment are now more restricted. Emigration has been a long standing feature but the area retains a relatively high population density and a youthful age structure. Improvement of local employment opportunities is a priority.

Conservation can go hand in hand with rural development. Imaginative approaches are needed to allow conservation to be a generator of local employment and income. The Ring of Gullion has unique 'products' to offer — its landscape, wildlife and heritage. Farming activity must continue to have a high profile but conservation can promote enjoyment of the countryside, and generate additional income from leisure and tourism.

Local collective action focussed around the parish, village and townland has deep roots in the area. Several energetic groups represent a wide range of interests, and these groups can be a useful mechanism for the delivery of an integrated approach to rural development.

3.13.2 POLICIES

- to retain a working rural population enthusiastic to conserve and promote the countryside;

- to achieve sustainable economic development following the principle of wise use;

- to provide the infrastructure and services necessary to facilitate rural development; and

- to support conservation as an economic activity.

3.13.3 ACTION

- to introduce a scheme of incentives for conservation work, including protection and management of semi-natural habitats, maintenance of field boundaries and gates, tree planting and maintenance of historic monuments and traditional farm buildings (Action: CWB, HMBB, DANI);

- to assist diversification of rural employment to provide long-term social and environmental benefits (Action: DANI, RDC, ROSA); and

- to develop a good working partnership between government departments and agencies for the support and guidance of local community groups (Action: RDC, DANI, HMBB, CWB, TCPS, NMDC).

Natural heath vegetation

Standard code of answers

NE New edition in preparation

NP Not yet published

OO On order abroad

RP Reprinting

TOS Temporarily out of stock

TF To follow

Your order has been recorded
and will be held for twelve
months; if at the end of
this period the publication
is not available you will
be notified

NA Currently not available. Your order has not been held.

NH Not published or sold by HMSO

OP Out of print, not to be reprinted.
Photocopies of out of print Parliamentary, Statutory and
Regulatory publications can be obtained by HMSO from
the British Library Document Supply Centre. Customers
requiring this service should order via HMSO (Photocopies),
PO Box 276, London SW8 5DT enclosing £4.35 inc. VAT per
complete copy required. Please allow 15 days for delivery.

RE Repealed

RV Revoked

SU Superseded

Enquiries

Address all enquiries to the address shown overleaf.
If the address is PO Box 276 the following enquiry
points should be used.

Enquiry Section
HMSO Books
51 Nine Elms Lane
London SW8 5DR
Telex: 297138 Fax: 071 873 8463
Telephone
071 873 0011 *(General enquiries)*
071 873 0022 *(Order enquiries)*
0800 282827 *(Free information line)*

Sales Invoice

⚜HMSO 49 High Holborn London   WC1V 6HB

Books

49 High Holborn London   WC1V 6HB

From HMSO Books

Invoice enclosed

For the attention of

MRS R PATTERSON
135 BALLYMORRAN ROAD
KILLINCHY
NEWTOWNARDS
BT23 6TT

Customer Reference   NONE   C984035

Conditions of supply, payment methods and useful information overleaf. Pay

Copies	Title	Ar co
1	0337082499 MOURNE Mountain Walks	
1	0337082871 Ring of Gullion: Area of outstanding natural beauty: guide to designation	

No returns will be accepted for credit unless
incorrectly or goods have been received damag
to return for credit must be obtained prior t

VAT registration No. GD245

Vat code	A	Total at	0.00	%
Vat code		Total at		%
Vat code		Total at		%
Vat code		Total at		%

CASH PAID

Printed in the UK for HMSO 8296782 7/92 C6000 10146 938 12181

PC100

o.   55175421   Page   1

t date: 16/11/92

No: CASH PAID

ef: C984035

er's ref: NONE

by

ASH RECEIVED WITH ORDER**
      THANK YOU (HOLBORN)   ****
1SO Bookshop
.gh Holborn
n
6HB

ue within 28 days of invoice date.

Price £ p	Discount %	VAT code	Total goods £ p
4.95		A	4.95
4.50		A	4.50
O has supplied Authorisation turning goods			

	Total goods excl. VAT	9.45
	Total VAT on invoice	0.00
5	**Total amount due £**	0.00

HMSO Bookshops

Belfast
16 Arthur Street
Belfast BT1 4GD

Tel: 0232 238451

National Giro
Acct. No. 678-3007

Northern Bank Ltd
Law Courts Branch
110 Victoria Street
Belfast BT1 3GN

Sort Code 95-01-31

Acct. No. 71040669

Birmingham
258 Broad Street
Birmingham B1 2HE

Tel: 021-643 3740

Bristol
33 Wine Street
Bristol BS1 2BQ

Tel: 0272 264306

Edinburgh
71 Lothian Road
Edinburgh EH3 9AZ

Tel: 031-228 4181

National Giro
Acct. No. 108-0318

London
49 High Holborn
London WC1V 6HB

Tel: 071-873 0011

Manchester
9/21 Princess Street
Manchester M60 8AS

Tel: 061-834 7201

National Giro
Acct. No. 613-1611

Payment instructions

Payments may be made at any HMSO Bookshop or se

The Cashier
HMSO Books
51 Nine Elms Lane
London SW8 5DR

Method of Payment

Post Cheques, Postal O
be sent to the abc
bookshop address
payable to HMSO
crossed Account F
must be accompan
details of all releva
Cheques from non
customers should I
payable in £ Sterlir
on a UK bank acco

Bank notes and co
not be sent throug

Girobank Pay via National Gi
No. 582-1002. The
account numbers r
quoted in the mess
on the Giro form

Bank Giro Credit **Title of Account**
HMSO Publications
No. 2 Account

Bank name/address Lloyds Bank plc
South Bank Branch
2 York Road
London SE1 7LZ

Bank sort code 30-18-25

Account number 0148733

A separate remittance advice giving
full details of invoice number(s) must
forwarded to HMSO at the address
where payment is made.

For Deposit Account Customers this invoice is
for information only.

Appendices

TOWNLANDS IN THE RING OF GULLION AONB

Fathom Upper
Fathom Lower
Clontygora
Ellisholding
Newtown
Ballymacdermot
Seafin
Carrivemaclone (part of)
Altnaveigh (part of)
Corrinshigo
Carrivekenny
Derry More (part of)
Carrickbrackan (part of)
Cross (part of)
Keggal
Ballinliss
Tamnaghbane
Clonlum
Meigh
Mullaghbane
Shanroe
Glebe
Maphoner
Carrickaldreen
Carrickbroad

Aughadanove
Ballykeel
Clarkill
Doctors Quarters
Carrickngalliagh
Aghmakane
Ballynalack
Lislea
Ummerinvore
Ballard
Carrigans
Killeen
Ballintemple
Levallymore
Foughill Etra
Foughill Otra
Edenappa
Aghadavoyle
Annahaia
Aghayalloge
Tievecrom
Carrickastickan
Shean
Cloghinny
Longfield

Carrive
Tullydonnell (O'Callaghan) (part of)
Tullydonnell (Gage) (part of)
Ballynaclosha (part of)
Cashel
Legmoylin (part of)
Tullynavall (part of)
Dorsy (part of)
Carrowmannan (part of)
Belleek (part of)
Drumilly (part of)
Tullyah (part of)
Duburren (part of)
Sturgan (part of)
Carrickcloghan (part of)
Slieve Gullion
Tullymacreeve
Latbirget
Annacloghmullin
Carnacally
Aughanduff
Ummeracam (Ball North)
Ummeracam (Ball South)
Carricknagavna
Cloghoge (part of)

GEOLOGICAL BACKGROUND

The rocks of the Ring of Gullion are complex and have puzzled scientists for many years. The oldest rocks in the area are Silurian greywackes, part of wide belt of sedimentary rocks stretching across Ireland from County Longford to County Down and extending across the Irish Sea into southern Scotland. Into these rocks, masses of granite were intruded, underlying the town of Newry and much of the Slieve Gullion area. To the west of Newry the contact between these 'Newry' granites and the Silurian rocks stretches in a large arc from Camlough to Silverbridge, Forkill and Fathom.

Much later in geological time, in the Tertiary period, this area once again became the centre of volcanic activity. The sequence of events is complex: volcanoes erupted in the south of the area and the remains of volcanic vents can be found in the hills around Forkill. Along the contact zone between the Silurian rocks and the Newry granite a roughly circular fracture developed into which was intruded acidic lava which cooled to form very hard granophyre and felsite rocks — the 'ring dyke'.

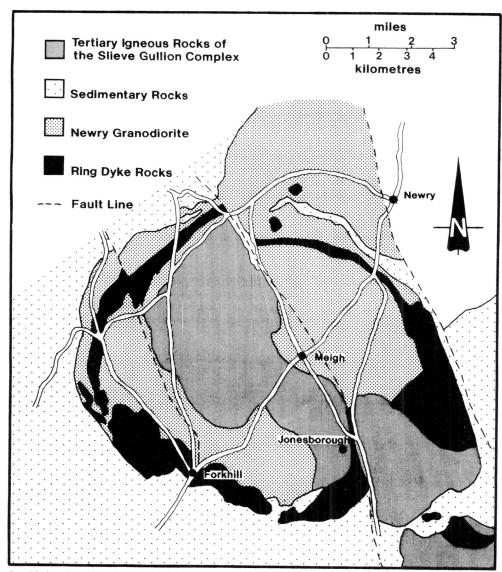

Simplified geology of the Ring of Gullion (based on Regional Geology of Northern Ireland H E Wilson, HMSO, 1972)

APPENDIX 2

Ring dyke in Cashel townland

Slieve Gullion itself is made up of layers of granitic and basaltic rocks and there has been some debate as to their origins. One suggestion is that a huge explosive eruption created a vast crater, or caldera, into which lavas were extruded in layers. Another more plausible explanation is that the lavas were intruded deep underground to be unearthed by subsequent erosion.

In the present landscape the hard rocks of the ring dyke remain outstanding as the circle of sharp, rugged hills — Sugarloaf Hill, Slievenacappel, Mullaghbane Mountain, Croslieve, Tievecrom, Slievebolea, Feede Mountain, Flagstaff, Fathom Mountain and Ballymacdermot Mountain. The central stack of hard granitic and basaltic rocks now forms the massive bulk of Slieve Gullion, whilst the older 'Newry' granite has been worn down to form the floor of the ring, between Slieve Gullion and the surrounding hills.

To the west the Silurian rocks underlie the drumlin plain which extends into the far distance towards Markethill, Keady and Castleblayney.

In more recent times the landscape has been shaped by the action of glaciers during successive Ice Ages. In the last glaciation an ice sheet, centred over mid-Ulster, flowed out across South Armagh towards the Irish Sea via Carlingford Lough and Dundalk Bay. Glaciers exploited existing weaknesses in the rocks (faults and softer rocks) to erode deep valleys through the Ring of Gullion -the Newry River, Camlough, Flurry River and Forkill River valleys. The protruding hills were glacially scoured leaving craggy outcrops, boulder strewn slopes, rocky ridges and hollows, while the valley bottoms were infilled with glacial deposits forming rounded drumlin ridges streamlined by the flowing ice. The 'tail' of Slieve Gullion at Drumintee is a remarkable ridge of boulder clay deposited in the wake of Slieve Gullion.

Rock fall, Slieve Gullion

(Source: Agricultural Census 1 June 1990, DANI Farm Census Branch[1])

Table 1 Livestock

Livestock	Number
Cattle & calves	17,604
Sheep & lambs	23,487
Goats	281
Horses	57
Pigs	2,249
Poultry	12,268

Table 2 Farm land use

Land Use	Holdings (ha)
Crops	137
Grass under 5 years old	2,046
Grass over 5 years old	5,873
Rough grazing	1,978
Woods	36
Other land	177
Total area of holdings	10,247

Table 3   Distribution of farms by business size and type

Business Type	Business Size			All sizes	
	Very Small	Small	Medium/Large	All Farms	Area (ha)
Dairying	14	43	5	62	1587
Mainly beef	192	57	3	252	5608
Mainly sheep	37	19	0	56	1270
Other types	7	6	1	14	194
Unclassified	119	—	—	119	1301
All types	369	125	9	503	9960

[1]Figures derived for Ring of Gullion by DANI Farm Census Branch based on addresses of farms lying within the AONB.

APPENDIX 3

APPENDIX 4

Number*	Townland	Site Type	Comment
1	Ballymacdermot	Court Tomb	
2	Ballykeel	Portal Tomb	
3	Slieve Gullion	Multiple Cist Cairn	North Cairn
4	Slieve Gullion	Passage Grave	South Cairn
5	Ballintemple	Churches	Killevy
6	Clonlum	Court Tomb	North (not managed)
7	Clonlum	Portal Tomb	South
8	Killeen	Cashel and Souterrain	Lisdoo (not managed)
9	Killeen	Cashel	Lisbanemore (not managed)
10	Clontygora	Court Tomb	
11	Carrickbroad	Tower and Bawn	Moyry Castle
12	Edenappa	Inscribed Stone and Graveyard	Kilnasaggart

*Numbers refer to map on Page 13.

ABBREVIATIONS USED IN SECTION 3

Newry and Mourne District Council

NMDC   Newry and Mourne District Council

Department of the Environment (NI)

ES	Environment Service
CWB	Countryside and Wildlife Branch
HMBB	Historic Monuments and Buildings Branch
EPD	Environmental Protection Division
WS	Water Service
RS	Roads Service
TCPS	Town and Country Planning Service

Department of Agriculture (NI)

DANI	Department of Agriculture (NI)
DANI(FS)	Forest Service of Department of Agriculture (NI)

Government Agencies

SELB	Southern Education and Library Board
NIE	Northern Ireland Electricity
NIHE	Northern Ireland Housing Executive
NITB	Northern Ireland Tourist Board
SCNI	Sports Council for Northern Ireland

RDC	Rural Development Council
CVNI	Conservation Volunteers
FWAG(NI)	Farming and Wildlife Advisory Group
TNI	Tidy Northern Ireland
NI2000	Northern Ireland 2000
ROSA	Regeneration of South Armagh

APPENDIX 5

GLOSSARY OF STATUTORY DESIGNATIONS

DEPARTMENT OF THE ENVIRONMENT (NI)

ENVIRONMENT SERVICE

COUNTRYSIDE AND WILDLIFE BRANCH

1. Areas of Outstanding Natural Beauty (AONBs)

Areas of Outstanding Natural Beauty are areas of countryside with exceptional qualities of landscape, heritage and wildlife. An AONB is designated by the Department as part of the process of protecting and conserving these qualities and promoting their enjoyment. It is intended to be a positive contribution to rural development.

The purpose of designation is to provide a framework within which the Department may agree policies and proposals for:-

a. conserving or enhancing the natural beauty and amenities of the area;

b. conserving wildlife, historic features or natural phenomena within it;

c. promoting its enjoyment by the public; and

d. providing and maintaining public access to it.

These policies and proposals are drawn up in consultation with the people of the area, the District Council and all other interested parties.

Within the AONB other public bodies, in the exercise of their statutory responsibilities, are obliged to give special consideration to the conservation of the countryside.

However, designation does not affect the ownership or occupation of the land and does not interfere with the duty and role of the District Council in the administration of the area.

AONBs are provided for by The Nature Conservation and Amenity Lands (NI) Order 1985.

2. Areas of Special Scientific Interest (ASSIs)

Areas of Special Scientific Interest are recognised as regionally, nationally or internationally important sites for nature conservation. They include the best examples of a range of habitats such as bogs, woodland and meadows, as well as sites of interest for their geology or for rare species. Their protection largely involves the maintenance of current management practices, and landowners are asked to consult the Department in proposals for certain land use or management changes. Management agreements allow for voluntary co-operation between landowners and the Department and, where necessary, compensating payments may be agreed. There is no automatic right of access to sites in private ownership.

ASSIs are identified and declared under the provisions of The Nature Conservation and Amenity Lands (NI) Order 1985.

3. National Nature Reserves (NNRs)

National Nature Reserves are nationally or internationally important sites representing the best examples of wildlife habitats existing in Northern Ireland. They are managed specifically to conserve nature and for education or research. While most have open access some are restricted due to the need for protection. Nearly all are in public ownership by the Department of the Environment or the Department of Agriculture, Forest Service.

Until the introduction of The Nature Conservation and Amenity Lands (NI) Order 1985 the appropriate legislation was the Amenity Lands Act (NI) 1965.

4. Other Nature Reserves

In addition to NNRs there are other sites of regional importance for nature conservation which may be especially suitable for education, research or public enjoyment. These Nature Reserves may be owned or leased and managed by the Department of the Environment, the Department of Agriculture, Forest Service, the District Councils and voluntary bodies such as the Ulster Wildlife Trust, the Royal Society for Protection of Birds and the National Trust. The Reserves are generally managed by agreement with the Department.

HISTORIC MONUMENTS AND BUILDINGS BRANCH

5. State Care Monuments

State Care sites are historic monuments which are owned or held in guardianship and maintained by the Department. The sites represent some of the most important and best preserved monuments in Northern Ireland. They are generally open to the public. Explanatory notices and facilities for visitors are often provided.

Acquisition and management of State Care sites is provided for by the Historic Monuments Act (NI) 1971.

6. Scheduled Monuments

Scheduled monuments are other important historic monuments and sites which although in private ownership are scheduled for protection under the Historic Monuments Act (NI) 1971. There is no right of access to most of these monuments and visitors are advised to seek the landowner's permission. Advice on all historic monuments and archaeological finds is provided by the Department. Most archaeological sites are not scheduled but this does not minimise their importance.

7. Listed Buildings

Listed buildings are buildings of special architectural or historic interest. Buildings are selected for listing by the Department with the advice of the Historic Buildings Council and the relevant District Council. Only a few listed buildings are open to the public on a regular basis. The Planning (NI) Order 1972 and The Planning and Buildings Regulations (Amendment) (NI)

Order 1990 set out the legal requirements relating to listing. All proposals for alteration or demolition, both partial and complete, must be first approved by the Department.

8. Conservation Areas

Conservation Areas are built-up areas of special architectural or historic interest, the character and appearance of which it is desirable to preserve and enhance. They are designated under the provisions of The Planning (NI) Order 1972.

DEPARTMENT OF AGRICULTURE

9. Environmentally Sensitive Areas (ESAs)

Environmentally Sensitive Area schemes are designed to help conserve those areas of high landscape and/or wildlife value which are vulnerable to changes in farming practices. Under the voluntary schemes payments are offered to farmers willing to maintain or convert to environmentally beneficial farming practices.

ESAs are designated under the provisions of The Agriculture (Environmental Areas) (NI) Order 1987.

APPENDIX 7

USEFUL ADDRESSES

NEWRY AND MOURNE DISTRICT COUNCIL

Newry and Mourne District Council
O'Hagan House
Monaghan Row
NEWRY
BT35 8DL
TEL: Newry 65411

DEPARTMENT OF THE ENVIRONMENT

ENVIRONMENT SERVICE

Countryside and Wildlife Branch
Calvert House
23 Castle Place
BELFAST BT1 1FY
TEL: Belfast 230560

Environmental Protection Division
Calvert House
23 Castle Place
BELFAST BT1 1FY
TEL: Belfast 230560

Historic Monuments and Buildings Branch
Hill Street
BELFAST BT1
TEL: Belfast 235000

TOWN AND COUNTRY PLANNING SERVICE

Craigavon Divisional Planning Office
Marlborough House
Central Way
CRAIGAVON
TEL: Craigavon 341144

ROADS SERVICE

Craigavon Divisional Office
Marlborough House
Central Way
CRAIGAVON
TEL: Craigavon 341144

WATER SERVICE

Southern Division Office
Marlborough House
Central Way
CRAIGAVON
TEL: Craigavon 341144

DEPARTMENT OF AGRICULTURE

Headquarters
Dundonald House
Upper Newtownards Road
BELFAST BT4 3SB
TEL: Belfast 650111

Armagh County Agricultural Executive
Office
2 Newry Road
ARMAGH
TEL: Armagh 524979

Watercourse Management Office
The Mall
ARMAGH
TEL: Armagh 522774

Forest Service
Down/Armagh District Office
The Grange
CASTLEWELLAN
TEL: Castlewellan 71144

GOVERNMENT AGENCIES

Southern Education & Library Board
3 Charlemont Place
ARMAGH
TEL: Armagh 523811

Northern Ireland Electricity
Danesfort
120 Malone Road
BELFAST
TEL: Belfast 661100

Northern Ireland Housing Executive
The Housing Centre
2 Adelaide Street
BELFAST BT2 8PB
TEL: Belfast 240588

Northern Ireland Tourist Board
St Anne's Court
59 North Streeet
BELFAST BT1 1NB
TEL: Belfast 231221

Sports Council for Northern Ireland
House of Sport
Upper Malone Road
BELFAST BT9 5LA
TEL: Belfast 381222

NON-GOVERNMENTAL AGENCIES

Rural Development Council
Loughry College of Agriculture
Loughry
COOKSTOWN
Co Tyrone BT80 9AA
TEL: Cookstown 62491

Conservation Volunteers
The Pavilion
Cherryvale Park
BELFAST BT6 0BZ
TEL: Belfast 645169

Farming and Wildlife Advisory Group
Hydebank
4 Hospital Road
BELFAST BT8 8JP
TEL: Belfast 647161

Ulster Wildlife Trust
New Line
CROSSGAR BT30 9EP
TEL: Crossgar 830282

The Tidy Northern Ireland Group
Philips House
123 York Street
BELFAST BT15 1AB
TEL: Belfast 328105

Northern Ireland 2000
Armagh House
Ormeau Avenue
BELFAST BT2 8HB
TEL: Belfast 238532

Regeneration of South Armagh
c/o Community Enterprise Centre
The Square
CROSSMAGLEN
Co. Armagh
TEL: Newry 861534

Text pages made with recycled fibres